Investing Guide for Beginners

Understanding Futures, Options, Stocks, Bonds, Bitcoins

By

Michael Brentwood

FREE BONUS: Click The Link Below To Receive Your

Bonus

https://publishfs.leadpages.co/pangea-health/

© **Copyright 2014 by** _____ **- All rights reserved.**

This document is geared towards providing exact and reliable information in regards to the topic and issue covered. The publication is sold with the idea that the publisher is not required to render accounting, officially permitted, or otherwise, qualified services. If advice is necessary, legal or professional, a practiced individual in the profession should be ordered.

- From a Declaration of Principles which was accepted and approved equally by a Committee of the American Bar Association and a Committee of Publishers and Associations.

In no way is it legal to reproduce, duplicate, or transmit any part of this document in either electronic means or in printed format. Recording of this publication is strictly prohibited and any storage of this document is not allowed unless with written permission from the publisher. All rights reserved.

The information provided herein is stated to be truthful and consistent, in that any liability, in terms of inattention or otherwise, by any usage or abuse of any policies, processes, or directions contained within is the solitary and utter responsibility of the recipient reader. Under no circumstances will any legal responsibility or blame be held against the publisher for any reparation, damages, or monetary loss due to the information herein, either directly or indirectly.

Respective authors own all copyrights not held by the publisher.

The information herein is offered for informational purposes solely, and is universal as so. The presentation of the information is without contract or any type of guarantee assurance.

The trademarks that are used are without any consent, and the publication of the trademark is without permission or backing by the trademark owner. All trademarks and brands within this book are for clarifying purposes only and are the owned by the owners themselves, not affiliated with this document.

INTRODUCTION

I want to thank you and congratulate you for downloading the book, *"Investing Guide for Beginners: How you can Prepare for your Future and Smartly?"*.

This book contains proven steps and strategies on how to be successful in investing.

Because times are hard, most people are afraid of the future. Most of them are worried that they won't have enough money to survive in the future. Some people see a bleak future because they do not know what will happen to them.

Fortunately, there is hope. You can still maintain your present lifestyle in the future, even if you already have your own family and have several responsibilities. It is not an easy task, though. Investing shows a great promise. In fact, there are people who have become successful in it. The great Warren Buffett is one great example. However, you need not be like him. You just have to take your first step towards investing, so that you can prepare for your unknown future.

This book can help you immensely. Kindly go through each

chapter thoroughly, so that you will understand some of the most important investing concepts. If you understand them fully, you can take that first confident step to prepare you financially for the future.

Thanks again for downloading this book, I hope you enjoy it!

Contents

INTRODUCTION

CHAPTER 1

Investing Principles Made Easy 1
- Reasons for Investing 2
- The Miracle of Compounding 3
- The Psychology of Investing 3

CHAPTER 2

Investment Account Principles 6
- Broker Fees to Consider 9
- Important Points to Consider in Selecting a Brokerage Firm 10

CHAPTER 3

Making Tax-Efficient Investment Decisions 13
- Types of Investment Account Based on Tax Efficiency 13
- The Income Tax Bracket 14
- Tax on Dividend Income 15
- Tax on Interest Income 16
- Tax on Income from Capital Gains 16
- Wash Sales and Tax Losses 17
- How to Lessen the Tax Burden? 18

CHAPTER 4

Creating a Personal Investment Plan 20
- How to Create a Personal Investment Plan 23
- Risk and Return Objectives 23

Investment Guidelines and Constraints 24

Investment Policy 25

Monitoring, Reevaluation, and Rebalancing of the Investment Portfolio 25

CHAPTER 5

The Alpha and Beta of Investing 26

The Alpha Ratio 26

The Beta Ratio 28

Reliance on Past Performance 29

How to Improve the Investment Portfolio Using Alpha and Beta? 29

Measuring Price Fluctuations Using Beta 31

CHAPTER 6

Learning about Asset Classes 33

Common Categories of Equities 34

How to Achieve Investing Success? 35

CHAPTER 7

Asset Allocation and Portfolio Diversification 37

Asset Allocation 38

The Relationship between Risk and Reward 39

The Beauty of Diversification 40

CHAPTER 8

Stocks – Basic Information 42

CHAPTER 9

Stocks Investing Tricks 51

Important Considerations about Stocks Investing 51

How to Check a Company's Fundamentals before Investing on its Stock? 53

Financial Formulas to Learn Before Investing in Stock 54

Reading List for All Stock Investors 54

Reassurance for Nervous Stock Investors 55

CHAPTER 10

Important Things to Remember about Options Trading 56

Order Types 56

Charts an Options Trader Can Use to Track His Investments 58

Construction of Financial Indexes 59

How Stocks Affect Indexes 59

CHAPTER 11

Principles of Futures Trading 61

Futures Market Categories 63

Types of Trade 65

CHAPTER 12

Trading Bitcoins 67

Bitcoin Basics 68

How to Buy Bitcoins? 69

How to Store Bitcoins 69

How to Secure Bitcoins 70

How to Mine Bitcoins 71

CHAPTER 13

The Federal Reserves 73

The structure 74

Duties and responsibilities 76

Controversies 79

CHAPTER 14

Lessons From Mutual Funds and University Endowments 83
- Mutual Funds 83
- University Endowments 85

CHAPTER 15

Good Debt Vs. Bad Debt 88
- Key characteristics of good debt 89
- Key characteristics of bad debt 89

CHAPTER 16

Teaching Your Children About Money 91
- Why Isn't Personal Finance Taught In School? 92
- What About The Good Schools? 95
- Tips For Effectively Teaching Your Children About Finances 96

CHAPTER 17

The Future Is Yours! 101

CONCLUSION *104*

Chapter 1

Investing Principles Made Easy

Investing is an activity which requires you to commit a specific amount of money to a particular investment product while also expecting to earn a huge return from it. Majority of individuals believed that the only way for them to make money is to get a job since this will allow them to earn decent income.

People fail to recognize that they have to extend their working hours if they want to earn more money. They have to find time for rest and relaxation with family and friends. It is common knowledge that people focused on earning money no longer have time for leisure. These hardworking individuals do not enjoy the fruits of their labor.

Fortunately, there is a way for you to earn more money by letting it work for you. Instead of working longer hours, you can use your money to maximize your earning potential. You can put it in real estate, bonds, stocks, mutual funds, or business.

Some people get confused between investing and gambling. They cannot differentiate the two. Gambling bets on uncertain results. Gamblers can only hope that they win in the end. Some people may liken investing to gambling. They may purchase an investment asset based on an unverified hot tip they heard from an officemate. They really do not perform due diligence.

True investing requires you to act. It does not want you to buy a random investment with your hard-earned money. It requires you to analyze the investment thoroughly and commit your money to it when you realize it is reasonable to expect profit from it. Investing does not guarantee profits because every investment has its risks. However, it does not rely on Lady Luck alone.

Reasons for Investing

First, people invest because they want more money. They want to gain personal financial freedom to afford the lifestyle they want. They want a sense of security.

Second, they decide to invest their money because they see a need for it. They become worried that they will not be receiving any fat pension when they retire. They need to have money to maintain their current lifestyle.

Third, they see a shift of retirement planning from the government to the individual, thus, there is a need to plan to ensure that they will be financially stable when they retire.

THE MIRACLE OF COMPOUNDING

Compounding is useful for everyone. Unlike other forms of mathematics, it can transform money into a powerful income-generating tool. Compounding generates more money from reinvested profits of an investment asset. For this to be true, it must include time and reinvested profits. It means that given more time, you can increase the income possibility of your investment when you reinvest the earnings you get from it.

For example, John invests $10,000 at 6% interest per annum. After year 1, he expects to have $10,600 in his investment account. He plans to leave the interest in his account. Therefore, after year 2, he expects his money to be worth $11,236. The $600 interest he left in his investment account earned $36. Although it may seem like a small amount, compounding allows the capital to earn more money over time.

THE PSYCHOLOGY OF INVESTING

You cannot dismiss psychology as a helpful tool in investing. Being more aware of how you think and react, as well as what biases affect your decision-making, can develop your skills in investing. If you don't control your emotions, you will experience denial, pride, fear, greed, or ego that can affect your investing decisions.

New investors believe that to be successful, they need to search for the right strategy and a good investment. However, doing these things does not guarantee success because even the most prepared investor may lose money if there is a major market correction. Any inexperienced investor will just let his emotion take control and watch his investment decimate in value because he is hoping that he will recover his losses someday.

Most investors do not want to lose money because that will be a painful experience for them. They will hold on to their losing investments, instead of selling them because they do not want to feel the pain. They allow their emotions to take control of their decisions. They believe that the investments will recover in due time.

This is the main reason why you should never include your emotions when investing. Take your time to study yourself, your flaws, and thinking process, so that you can develop the skills to fight the negative psychological effects to your investments.

Avoid attaching yourself emotionally to any of your investments because this may cause you to ignore anything negative about them. In addition, you will also most likely ignore money management rules. Not using your head can damage your financial status, thus, you need to strive to be aware of your investment plan at all times. This can help you make sound investing decisions in a more disciplined, focused, and calmer way.

Learn to accept that you cannot be successful every time. It is possible for you to experience losses, sometimes. Know the acceptable maximum loss you can take before investing your money. This maximum loss amount must be something that you can accept. Learn more about risk management, so that your losses will always be lesser than your profits.

If you are still a new investor, you may search for a good investing book and follows its strategies. You may have some winning moments but after a few losses, you tend to abandon the strategies and begin search for another book. Avoid committing this mistake. Instead of abandoning your strategies, make a thorough analysis and find out what went wrong. For you to be successful, it is necessary to recognize your mistakes and correct them. Accept the fact that there is no Holy Grail in investing.

Chapter 2

Investment Account Principles

Before opening an investment account, you need to know your investment requirements and objectives, especially if you are still a beginner. Learn more about yourself since it is also the key to finding the most suitable broker or brokerage firm for you.

A brokerage firm is a business, which connects an investor and his actual investments. It transacts investment assets for its clients. As an investor, you must know which one between the discount broker and a full service broker can benefit you the most.

A full service broker provides face-to-face contact. You can visit the broker's office and talk to a representative to help you with your investments. Usually, you will have your own representative to handle your investment account. You can contact this representative anytime.

A full service broker is a good choice if you are still a new and inexperienced investor. It charges higher fees than a discount broker does. Note, however, that there are unscrupulous full service brokers who may suggest expensive investments, so they can collect higher fees. Some full service brokers are not also knowledgeable about a certain transaction, so there is a great chance that they will convince an investor not to do it.

A discount broker, on the other hand, is ideal for you if you already have basic knowledge and some experience in investing. It allows you to use an investing platform online, so you can do certain transactions by yourself. It charges lower fees because it offers minimum help only. It can charge a low $5 commission per transaction.

Many online brokerage firms are also discount brokers. However, these companies offer varying services and quality of customer support. You can still to talk to a customer service representative, but these brokerage firms may charge a fee for the service. Make sure to check different brokerage firms and find out which one will work effectively for you before signing up with one of them.

You can visit the website of your chosen broker to open an investment account. Provide some personal information in the application form. Most websites are user-friendly, so you just need to follow the instructions when signing up for an investment account.

You also need to choose the right investment account, which perfectly meets your trading requirements. Determine your risk tolerance level after deciding on the broker type. Your chosen broker will ask you about your risk tolerance level, so that he can determine the best investment account for you.

Risk can be conservation of capital, income, growth or speculative. If you are an investor who wants to take long positions (traditional purchase of assets), then you can assume the first three risks mentioned when you dabble into more advanced transactions, like options trading or shorting of assets.

After determining your risk tolerance level, you need to decide on the type of investment account you want. You can choose from the popular types like cash and margin, and cash only. It is important to understand each type of accounts.

Each type of account can have its own tax status. After choosing the investment account type, you need to choose its tax status. You can opt for a retirement or a traditional broker account. A retirement account (Individual Retirement Account, Roth Individual Retirement Account, etc.) has more restrictions because of the tax treatments. It is best to discuss your choice with a tax advisor.

A taxable account must pay capital gains taxes when you decide to sell your assets. It is also necessary to pay tax on cash dividends issued by companies. However, money from the taxable account is liquid. You don't have to pay special penalties when you decide to sell your assets in it.

A special retirement account, on the other hand, makes it easier for you to save money for your retirement. Usually, you can delay paying taxes on your investment profits and contributions if you put your money in a special retirement account.

You can have two weeks, at most, to fund your chosen investment account. You may either send a check through the snail mail or deposit the money through wire transfer. Some brokers offer banking services. They may also offer debit cards connected to the investment account.

BROKER FEES TO CONSIDER

Aside from transaction fees, you need to know about other broker fees. If you are still young, you may have a limited budget, so you have to look into these fees to ensure that you make the most out of your money.

Many brokers set a minimum account balance. Usually, the amount can range from $500 to $1,000. This means that the broker has to ensure that your investment account balance does not fall below this limit to prevent penalties.

Used for leveraging, a margin account is a special account offered by brokers. An investor who wants to use leveraging must know that this account has a higher minimum balance requirement and charges a higher fee.

Some brokers also charge a fee if you want to withdraw money from your account. They may also not allow withdrawal if the investment account balance falls below the minimum balance requirement. It is important to know the withdrawal rules before signing up with a particular brokerage firm.

Some brokers also charge hidden fees. They may present a lower fee structure to encourage investors to sign up with them. As such, it is important to perform due diligence when choosing a broker. Ensure that the broker's fee structure matches your investing style.

Important Points to Consider in Selecting a Brokerage Firm

It is advisable to start with a full service broker if you are still on the stage of building up your knowledge and confidence in the field of investing. As you become more knowledgeable, you can shift to a discount broker.

Ensure that the broker's website does not encounter problems, especially during trading hours. Be mindful of broken links and the speed of loading the pages.

Another important thing to do is to check if the brokerage firm offers other options for placing orders. Inquire about fax ordering, telephone trades, or ordering from a broker representative over the phone. Ask about the prices for each option. It is also advisable to exercise due diligence when studying the offers of each brokerage firm in your list, so you can pick the best choice.

Be careful about signing up with a brokerage firm who offers low commission. There are instances when you need to pay higher fees for other important transactions not included in the low commission advertisement.

Another tip is to sign up with a brokerage firm, which advertises low initial deposit. In most cases, brokerage firms will allow a low initial deposit, but require high minimum balances.

Ensure that the brokerage firm offers various investment

products like certificates of deposits, futures, municipal bonds, commodities and options. This will allow you to have several investment options.

Your chosen broker representative should also be someone whom you can ask for help anytime. Look for a brokerage firm with a quick response time whenever you call them up to raise a question or concern.

Also, ask the brokerage firm about the interest rate they offer on idle cash left in the investment account. Note that while other brokers charge an interest, there are also those that don't. Another thing that you have to clarify with a broker is if they offer extra services. Find out if these extra services come with a fee. This will allow you to determine if the broker offers his services at reasonable cost.

CHAPTER 3

MAKING TAX-EFFICIENT INVESTMENT DECISIONS

A tax-efficient investment maximizes profits. In the US, there are complex tax laws pertaining to investments, so majority of investors don't understand how to make their portfolio tax efficient. The more money left after taxes, the more tax efficient an investment is. An investment is tax inefficient if it relies heavily on investment income, instead of its price movement.

TYPES OF INVESTMENT ACCOUNT BASED ON TAX EFFICIENCY

As an investor, it is crucial to learn the structure of your investment account, so you will know how to make it tax efficient. In general, an investment account can be tax exempt, tax deferred, or taxable.

You can pay income taxes during the taxable year you receive income from your taxable investment account. You can also delay payment of taxes on a tax-deferred investment account as long as you don't withdraw money from it. In some countries, an investor does not pay taxes on a tax-exempt account even if he withdraws money. In general, it is crucial to place your tax-efficient investments in a taxable account and your tax-inefficient investments in a tax-exempt or tax-deferred account.

THE INCOME TAX BRACKET

Knowing your marginal income tax bracket, and determining if this bracket is subject to the alternative minimum tax, is important in investing. If your income bracket is high, ensure that your investment accounts are tax-efficient. For example, if your income tax bracket is 39.65%, you can generate more benefits from a tax efficient investment account than someone who belongs to the 15% bracket.

After knowing the tax bracket, you have to be aware of the difference between capital gains tax and income tax. If you sold the asset after a year of owning it, you can pay tax on the profit from the sale using a preferential rate. On the other hand, if you sold the asset within the year, you can pay tax based on the marginal income tax bracket. To save on taxes, make sure to sell your investment assets after holding them for at least a year.

In some countries like the US, taxes differ based on the asset class. Interest income from bonds is taxable, except for the tax-efficient municipal bonds. If you belong to a higher income tax bracket, you will realize that bond investing is tax inefficient. As a rule, you must have a tax-deferred investment account for your tax-inefficient investments and a taxable account for your tax-efficient assets.

TAX ON DIVIDEND INCOME

A company can distribute dividends from its after-tax profit. This means that you don't need to pay taxes on qualified dividends if the company is in the US or in a country with a double-taxation treaty with the US. However, you have to pay ordinary income tax on non-qualified dividends. You can take advantage of the 15% preferential tax rate if you hold onto your share for at least 61 days before the ex-dividend date.

Example: An investor with a marginal income tax rate of 28% receives $500 as a qualified dividend on a stock he has in a taxable account for many years. He owes $75 in tax for it. However, for a non-qualified dividend of $500, he pays a tax of $140. He also has to pay the same amount if he does not hold the stock for at least one year. If he is a top-rate taxpayer, he has to pay $217 on the non-qualified dividend he received.

Tax on Interest Income

It is mandatory to pay ordinary income tax on interest earned from bonds. However, you don't need to include municipal bonds issued by US municipalities and bonds. You may pay the alternative minimum tax, though. Before buying a municipal bond, check the bond's federal tax status. There are cases when you don't need to pay state income taxes on interest earned from US Treasury securities.

Example: An investor receives a semi-annual interest of $1,000 for his $40,000 corporate bond. He needs to pay $330 income tax if his marginal income tax rate is 33%. However, he need not pay any federal tax on an $800 interest he received from his $40,000 municipal bond investment.

Usually, a top-rate taxpayer invests in municipal bonds in a taxable account to take advantage of the tax-exempt status even if these bonds have a lower yield.

Tax on Income from Capital Gains

If you hold an investment for at least one year, you can pay 15% capital gains tax when you sell it for profit. If you are a top-rate taxpayer, you need to pay 23.8% capital gains tax and healthcare surtax.

Example: An investor sold 100 shares of stock for a profit of $30 per share after one year of holding them. He has to pay $450 capital gains tax for the sale. On the other hand, if he sold them within the year, he has to pay $750 ordinary income tax for the sale if he belongs to the 25% tax bracket. If he is a top-rate taxpayer, he pays $450 if he held the share for at least year and $1,302 if he sold them within the year of purchase.

WASH SALES AND TAX LOSSES

You can offset your capital losses from your capital gains during the same taxable year. You can deduct a maximum of $3,000 net losses against your other taxable income during the taxable year. In addition, if losses are more than $3,000, you can offset them against gains in the future.

It is also possible to reduce your tax liability on capital gains by harvesting tax losses. If there are assets that drop in value below their costs, you can dispose these assets to realize the capital losses within the taxable year or future years. However, the Internal Revenue Service does not allow repurchase of a "substantially identical" asset within a month of the wash sale during the taxable year.

Example: An investor sold 100 shares of stock for a $20 loss per share. He also sold 100 shares of another stock for a gain of $70 per share. His taxable net gain is $5,000. If his tax bracket is 35%

and he held the other stock for at least a year, he pays $750 tax on his capital gains. However, if he sold the asset within a year after purchase, he pays $1,750 tax on his gains.

He cannot buy back the 100 shares of stock that he sold at a loss within 30 days if he does not want to pay tax on the full $7,000 capital gains tax.

How to Lessen the Tax Burden?

There are actually several ways to reduce your tax burden. One is to harvest tax losses by selling losing investment assets in a tax account to realize the losses. You can do this before the taxable year ends. This is an effective strategy if you want to offset capital gains on other investments.

You also have the option to use asset allocation strategies, so you can put some investments on particular accounts, thereby saving on taxes along the process. For long-term investments, place the assets in taxable accounts, so you can benefit from the preferential capital gains tax rate. You may also put mutual funds, exchange-traded funds and stocks that distribute qualified dividends to taxable account. Savings, individual and municipal bonds also go to taxable accounts.

Placing short-term stock investments, actively managed mutual funds, exchange-traded-funds that generate short-term gains, and high-yield bond funds and taxable bond funds to a tax-deferred investment account can also help. Furthermore, your investments in real estate investment trusts and zero-coupon bonds can also go to a tax-deferred account.

Another tip to reduce your tax burden is to pay more tax in actively managed funds because they have more turnovers within the taxable year. If you want to save on taxes, invest in passively managed exchange-traded funds or index funds.

Making a charitable donation of appreciated assets, like mutual funds, exchange-traded funds and individual stocks, is also a huge help in minimizing tax burden. You may receive credit for the donation if you hold the asset for at least a year. There is also no need to pay capital gains tax on the donated asset.

You can rebalance your investment portfolio to save on taxes. However, it is advisable to get the services of a skilled financial advisor to benefit fully from this scheme.

CHAPTER 4

CREATING A PERSONAL INVESTMENT PLAN

If you are still a new investor, knowing about your strengths and weaknesses can help you succeed. Understanding investments is a difficult task, but you need to spend time and effort to ensure that your money grows. By knowing your strengths and weaknesses, you will know exactly where you should invest your money and what you should avoid.

Understanding yourself involves learning how much risk you are willing to take once you start investing. A young person may tend to take more risks although most of them don't think of investing yet. However, note that you will most likely have healthy and happy retirement if you start funding your retirement account, like an Individual Retirement Account or 401(k), when you are still young.

Creating your time horizon is also necessary in successful investing. If you still have at least 25 years to invest your money, you may consider putting it on riskier investments. Still, it is crucial to exercise caution during the decision-making process. Invest in the stock market because it has earned higher returns historically although it is more volatile.

If you are not knowledgeable about investments, you can make an asset allocation plan consistent with your age then invest on some managed funds initially.

It is also advisable to know what you currently own. Check the recent statement of accounts of your present assets. If you are already investing, know how much your investments are currently worth, then decide on how much more capital you have to add for personal investing.

Decide on a timeframe for your investments. For example, if you want to invest in stocks, commit more hours per week to monitor the stocks, the companies, and the economy. Initially, you can buy a few stocks then commit about five hours per week to monitor and study the stock market. If you add more stocks, then you also need to spend more time for research.

Learning where to get the right information about your investments is also crucial for your success. You don't have to avail of expensive data services to analyze stocks. Usually, you can easily find reliable information from various online sources for free. These sources include the company's website for its financial reports and press releases, the SEC website for the company's filings, and the news sites for economic news and press releases.

Find some trusted sites and save the links on your web browser so you can easily access the information when needed. A reputable website informs its readers where it sources its data and how it updates the data to keep information accurate and current.

You also need to develop a strategy that you can easily follow through. It is beneficial to create a base asset allocation with exchange-traded funds or mutual funds. This way, you will feel less pressure because you no longer have to choose the assets in your portfolio.

In addition, you can decide on a specific asset class or sector/industry that interests you the most. Study it thoroughly and manage a part of your portfolio consisting of these assets more directly. However, it is not wise to put a lot of money in it. For example, you can check the S&P 500 index for its sector breakdown. If the index allots 15% to technology stocks, it is not wise to invest 60% of your portfolio in them.

Monitor the stocks that capture your interest. You can review them regularly for changes, and decide to sell some assets in the future and replace them with the stocks you are monitoring.

Schedule a regular review of your strategies. Monitor your progress against a benchmark, so you can make adjustments if necessary. This ensures progress in your attempt to learn on investments. For example, upon review, you found out that your portfolio has become out of balance because your stock investment grew significantly.

In this case, you can either put more money in some of your assets or sell some of the stocks to bring back the asset allocation percentages on their original state. Since the portfolio grew, realize that you have to spend more time to understand your investments.

Also, keep in mind that you will be learning many things in your journey. It may even take years for you to grow in experience. However, if you continue, you will find the whole journey enriching. You can decide to invest on other asset classes after achieving experience and expertise in investing.

How to Create a Personal Investment Plan

Risk and Return Objectives

In this part of the investment plan, you need to describe your profit expectations on your investments, so finding the best asset allocation strategies will be easier for you. This part of the plan will also describe how you should address investment risks.

Avoid dabbling into investing if you have no specific objectives yet. Determine how much return you expect from your investment portfolio during a specific period. Although you won't have a hundred percent guarantee when it comes to actual returns, your estimates can be a goal you can try to achieve during the specific period.

For example, if your expected yearly return is just 1% to 2%, you can invest in low-risk investments. If your expected annual return is between 5% and 8%, you can invest in moderate-risk investment. Invest in high-risk investments if you want to have an annual return of at least 9%.

INVESTMENT GUIDELINES AND CONSTRAINTS

Develop some investment guidelines and constraints as part of your investment plan. Investment guidelines serve as your roadmap to success. They can explain how you should invest on each of your life stages. If you are younger than 55 years old, you may decide to accumulate and grow your capital.

However, if you are nearing retirement age, you can opt for

wealth preservation. Lastly, the last stage is retirement wherein you already stopped working, so you no longer have a regular income. This is the stage when you rely on money you have accumulated from your investments.

Investment constraints are factors you have to consider when managing your investment portfolio. You must be capable of managing important constraints, like tax considerations, liquidity, special needs and time horizon.

INVESTMENT POLICY

The investment policy is the part of the investment plan, which includes acceptable and unacceptable investments, investment benchmarks, asset allocation plan, investment strategy, funding plan, and new investment strategy.

MONITORING, REEVALUATION, AND REBALANCING OF THE INVESTMENT PORTFOLIO

Lastly, you must include the means through which you will monitor, reevaluate, and balance your investment portfolio.

Chapter 5

The Alpha and Beta of Investing

Both alpha and beta are risk ratios that you may use to compute, compare and estimate profits. Usually, mutual funds use these ratios that utilize known market indexes like the S&P 500. These funds compare the performance of the index with an individual asset to know how this particular security will perform. The alpha and beta ratios are part of the standard risk computations that also include the Sharpe ratio, R-squared and standard deviation.

The Alpha Ratio

The alpha ratio is a measure of the aptitude of the portfolio manager. For instance, the mutual fund's growth of 8% is impressive if the overall return of the benchmark index is 4%. Its growth is less impressive if the other investments provide a return of 15%. In the first example, the portfolio manager has a higher alpha than the second one.

On the other hand, if the return of the investment portfolio is 3% when an investor expects it to earn 5% using the capital asset pricing model, the alpha ratio is -2%. In general, an investor prefers a higher alpha for any of his investments.

The formula for alpha = (end_price + dist_per_share - start_price) / (start_price)

A high alpha means that the portfolio manager is good in making investing decisions in behalf of the mutual fund's investors. However, the issue is if the alpha returns a positive number based on a particular benchmark, it is possible that this benchmark will be inappropriate to use.

For example, the portfolio manager reports an alpha of five based on the S&P 500 return of 15%. If he puts all the money on the Apple stock on August 1, 2014, he should have used the Apple performance of 18.14% as benchmark instead of the S&P 500 performance of 6.13%. This way, the alpha should have been about 1.86 instead of 13.87.

Experts, however, will not use the S&P index in comparing the Apple's performance. A more appropriate benchmark will be the NASDAQ, which returned 15.51% during 2014. This means that the portfolio manager should have reported an alpha of 4.49.

The Beta Ratio

Beta is a measure of an investment asset's volatility by comparing it with a particular benchmark for a period. You can use beta to learn about the expected amount of downside capture of an investment. Beta's baseline number is one while alpha's baseline number is zero.

If beta is equal to one, the price of a particular asset goes in the same direction as the market. On the other hand, if the beta is greater than one, the price of the asset is more volatile than the market. It is more difficult to evaluate beta than the alpha. A risk-averse investor wants a lower beta. However, some investors also want a higher beta, so that they can generate higher profits because of higher volatility.

Actually, beta is a multiplier. An investment asset, with a beta of two relative to a specific benchmark, means that its return can go up or down twice as much as that benchmark for a specific period. If the beta is -2, it means that the asset return goes in the opposite direction of the benchmark by a factor of two.

Furthermore, the beta is a measure of risk that you cannot eliminate by diversification. You need to exercise caution in relying solely on beta because its efficiency and effectiveness depends on the appropriate benchmark used.

RELIANCE ON PAST PERFORMANCE

Computations for alpha and beta involve historical data. Although historical performance does not guarantee that the investment will perform the same in the future, alpha and beta are helpful in differentiating between good and poor investments for a particular period.

HOW TO IMPROVE THE INVESTMENT PORTFOLIO USING ALPHA AND BETA?

You can separate your investment portfolio into alpha and beta portfolios, so that you can control your risk exposure effectively. You can also select your alpha and beta exposures to enhance returns.

The alpha-beta framework is a measurement of portfolio returns. Derived using linear regression analyzing, it compares the portfolio return with the index return for a particular period. The beta in the line equation is the slope of the line while the alpha is its y-intercept.

A beta exposure is an inherent component of your portfolio. It is not a fixed value for a given period. It is a systematic risk without a steady value. It is possible for you to separate the beta component to enhance the investment returns in relation to your level of risk tolerance.

Choose a market index as benchmark before selecting your beta exposure. In the US, the S&P 500 index is the gauge of movement in the market. However, you can also choose other benchmark if you think that the S&P 500 index does not represent the market accurately.

Next, you can select your portfolio's beta exposure. If you invest your investment capital in an S&P 500 index fund, your beta exposure will be equivalent to 0.5. The choice of a beta exposure is your personal decision.

It is also possible to get beta exposure by buying a futures contract, an index fund, or both. If you opt to buy an index fund, you must use a lot of money to enter a position. However, there is no limitation on the time horizon if you decide to take this option. On the other hand, if you buy a futures contract, you need less money to control an index fund's position. This option, however, has a settlement date and the transaction cost is expensive.

A pure alpha exposure means that the investment's returns are independent from the beta-derived returns using strategies like selling liquidity premiums in the market, equity neutral hedged strategies, statistical arbitrage, and the likes. A portfolio manager may buy individual assets for its alpha portfolio. Although this decision will not result to a pure alpha portfolio, you can use your skill to choose the assets that will result to a positive alpha.

You can also use the same strategy. A large hedge fund can only create a purely alpha portfolio because professionals run the fun with a lot of capital for the strategy.

MEASURING PRICE FLUCTUATIONS USING BETA

Many investors do not want to lose money so they choose low volatility investments. Other investors take more risks because they want to generate more profits. You need to thoroughly understand your level of risk tolerance and the investments that you can buy to match your risk preference.

Using beta, you can select investment assets that match your risk criteria. If you are a risk-averse investor, you can invest in low beta accounts like treasury bills and utility stocks. If you are willing to take on more risks, you can invest on securities with higher betas. Most brokers compute the betas of investments assets that they offer. However, most investors do not have access to them.

Other sources provide betas of securities like Yahoo Finance. A zero beta means that the security has no beta yet or is a new issue. The basis of the beta computation is the security's historical performance. Beta cannot predict future volatility. However, in a study by Gene Fama and Ken French, the beta reverts to the mean.

Another problem with beta is that it measures systematic risk, which is the overall market risk and not a specific asset risk. As such, you cannot rely on beta when it comes to looking into all the other risks you may face when investing in a particular asset.

CHAPTER 6

LEARNING ABOUT ASSET CLASSES

An asset class is a group of investment securities with the same characteristics, rules and regulations, and behavior in the marketplace. There are three major asset classes - cash equivalents, fixed income and equities. Some investment experts add commodities, hedge funds, art, private equity and real estate, collectively known as alternative investments, in the asset mix.

Cash equivalents include short-term liquid assets and cash. As the most stable asset class, you can opt to invest in commercial paper, government-issued securities, banker's acceptances, euros, and certificates of deposits. Fixed income investments are those securities that offer a fixed profit yearly for a certain period. Examples of fixed income include annuities and bonds.

Equities, on the other hand, are shares of stock of publicly owned corporations. Investors earn from the price movement of the stock. Equities provide the highest profit, but are also the most volatile. Typically, an investor must have various asset classes in his portfolio to mitigate the overall volatility.

COMMON CATEGORIES OF EQUITIES

A growth stock is a more expensive investment because it offers the best potential to grow significantly in the future. Investors put their money in startup stocks because of their high potential for growth even if they have negative earnings at present.

A value stock is a low price investment with low risks. Oftentimes, it provides high dividend yield. Investors do not expect the price of the stock to go up significantly.

In terms of location, a stock can be local, foreign, or foreign emerging. The first two stocks are self-explanatory while a foreign emerging stock is a stock from an undeveloped economy with higher expected returns, but is more volatile.

In terms of market capitalization, a stock can be small-cap, mid-cap, or large cap. A market capitalization is the total value of the stock. If the market capitalization exceeds $5 billion, the stock is large-cap. If the market cap is between $1B and $5B, the stock is mid-cap. Lastly, if the market capitalization is below $1B, it is a small-cap. A micro-cap is a stock with less than $300 million market capitalization.

Market capitalization is important in diversifying investment portfolio. Large companies are less risky and more stable than the smaller ones. However, smaller companies have the potential to grow more significantly in the future.

HOW TO ACHIEVE INVESTING SUCCESS?

First, you need to choose investments that comprise your asset class mix. In general, as you get older, you have to limit your risks because you may not have enough time to recover significant losses. To find out how much you have to invest in stocks, you can subtract your present age from 110. The remainder should be the portfolio percentage you must allot in stocks. The rest of the money should be in bonds.

For example, if you are 40 years old, you can put 70% of your capital in stocks and 30% in bonds. If you have other assets and cash, you can allocate 60% of your money in stocks, 25% in bonds, 10% in other investments, and 5% in cash. It is important not to put too much cash in the portfolio because inflation will just eat up its value.

For the stocks, decide the allocation of funds between growth and value stocks, and large-cap and small-cap stocks.

Second, you need to decide if you are going to be a passive or active investor. If you want to be a passive investor, you just need to select an index fund, which fits your needs. Otherwise, you have to choose your stocks wisely or hire the services of a professional to do it for you.

Actively managed mutual funds do not really outperform the market. You can choose stocks, but you need to ensure that your choices follow your asset allocation strategy. The goal is not to beat the market but to do well without losing a lot of money. In addition, you need to know the exact fees you have to pay. Find the most cost-effective investments so that you can lock in most of your profits.

Third, make sure to control your emotions and not let them ruin your investing plan. You may be tempted to dispose your holdings just because they are not making money, or buy hot stocks because you think that you can make more money from them. The most important thing is to spend time researching about your investments and be confident of your investing decisions.

Chapter 7

Asset Allocation and Portfolio Diversification

One of the reasons why you would like to diversify your portfolio is because you want to manage your risks more effectively by spreading your money on various assets. You can actually diversify within a particular asset class or across all asset classes, or do both the same time.

For example, you only invest your money in the stock market. If you want to diversify your portfolio, you can allocate your money to various stock sectors or industries. Divide one asset class into various subclasses. You can also choose stocks based on market capitalizations. Include stocks from various economic sectors.

Diversification allows you to mitigate non-systematic risks by using the strength of various subclasses to perform better over time. For example, you may invest in bonds with different maturity dates. You mitigate the risks by ensuring that a part of the portfolio can provide a stronger return.

Asset classes have limitations in terms of number. However, individual investments are almost unlimited. So far, no single diversification strategy can manage risk effectively. Diversification depends on how close the asset classes, individual investments and their potential returns correlate with each other.

Many investors opt to invest in mutual funds, variable annuities and exchange-traded funds to build a diversified portfolio easily. These pooled investments usually have large capitalization with various underlying assets to spread the risks. However, you need to ensure that these pooled investments follow a diversification strategy.

It is crucial to study asset allocation and diversification carefully before establishing your own investment portfolio. In addition, spend time monitoring your choices actively, so you can make all the necessary changes.

ASSET ALLOCATION

As a new investor, learning about the basic principles of sound investing is a must. Actually, you already know some of them through real-life and ordinary experiences. For example, you may notice a street vendor selling both sunglasses and umbrellas at the same time. Some people may find the idea ridiculous because no one will buy both items at the same time. However, the street vendor is reducing his risks by diversifying his products.

Asset allocation is a strategy of dividing the portfolio into different asset categories. It determines which asset mix will be in the portfolio. You can base your decision on time horizon and risk tolerance. If you have a longer time horizon, you can invest in riskier investments because you have more time to recover the losses. However, if you need the money to pay for your child's college education in a few years, then taking on less risky investments is a viable move.

The level of risk tolerance depends on your ability and willingness to lose money for possible greater gains. If you are aggressive, you may likely have a higher tolerance towards risks. On the other hand, if you are conservative, you will probably shy away from riskier investments.

THE RELATIONSHIP BETWEEN RISK AND REWARD

Every investment has its risks and rewards. If you want to buy investment assets, then you need to understand each one before making a decision. Note that those who take on more risks will most likely receive more rewards, while those who take on fewer risks will most likely generate fewer rewards. Instead of restricting your investments to less risky assets, invest in riskier assets if you have a long time horizon; otherwise, you can put your money in cash equivalents.

Asset allocation is important in protecting you against huge losses. Most major asset categories complement each other. They do not go up or down at the same time. An asset category may perform well during the prevailing market conditions while the others can only provide average or poor returns. Investing on at least one asset class can reduce your investment risk.

THE BEAUTY OF DIVERSIFICATION

Diversification is the process of spreading the funds into various investments to reduce the risks. You have to choose the right investments, so that you can minimize your losses and maximize your profits.

It is important to have the proper asset allocation model that meets your financial goal. This is not an easy task because you have to choose the asset mix, which allows you to match your financial goals at a manageable risks level. Hire the services of a financial professional to help you set up your asset mix. However, before doing so, you need to perform due diligence in finding the best financial advisor.

Some investors may use asset allocation as a tool to diversify their portfolio. However, most investors do not. Some invest solely on stocks or cash equivalents because of some particular circumstances. These investing decisions do not necessarily diversify the portfolio.

A wise investor diversifies within and between asset categories. This means allocating investments on various stocks, cash equivalents, bonds, and other assets to spread out your capital. It is important to determine the assets in every asset class because these assets have different performance under various market conditions.

Chapter 8

Stocks – Basic Information

Before you start implementation of your investment plans, be sure to check all information about the important aspects that relate to your investment. One such aspect is stocks or the stock market. The following part of this book will introduce you to the basic information about the stock market and stocks.

If we could offer you a definition of what stock actually is it may say something like this. Stocks, in many aspects, can be characterized as some sort of ownership over certain companies. The more stocks you own of some company the percentage of your ownership of that companies is higher.

When you buy stocks of some company, it means that you have a right to a certain amount of company's income and a part of what company has earned during a certain period of time. However, even if you own a certain amount of stocks of some company it does not mean that you have a right to participate in the decision making about the business. The range of your rights as a stock owner is limited to electing boards and naming CEOs and some other positions.

When you buy stock, and the transaction is completed, you should receive a stock certificate. This is sometime due to the fact that you can be an owner of stocks of some companies with whose business you are totally unfamiliar with. With this being said it is also important to mention the other side of the coin as well. With the limited range of decision making, you, as an owner of a certain amount of stock, are not responsible and liable for the business decisions or when and if it happens that the company whose stocks you own cannot fulfill their duties or pay off the debts.

This stock certificate serves as proof that you are the owner of the given stock, and this stock certificate is legally obliging. However, since technology made a huge leap in development in the recent period, in the majority of cases this stock certificate will not arrive at your home or business address. In that case, all records of your transactions, of your buying or selling of the stocks, will be recorded by your broker will record it electronically.

There is no need to worry because these electronic records have the same function as the stock certificate written on paper. When you own a certain amount of stocks of some companies, you are one of several, and often many, people who also own stocks of that company and in that way a network of stock owners or shareholders is created. Buying and selling of these stocks happen in stocks markets. Some of the most famous stocks markets are New York Stock Exchange – located in New York, USA; NASDAQ – located in USA, London Stock Exchange – located in the United Kingdom and Tokyo Stock Exchange – located in Japan.

It is also very important to emphasize that when someone is mentioning stocks, shares or equities they are all referring to the same thing. Those are just different names for the same thing. The biggest amount of trading that happens on stock markets happen on the floor as in the previously mentioned location. However, with the development of technology, virtual trade markets are becoming more and more popular.

The stock market can be characterized as a very complex system in which companies issue their shares or stocks. Besides issuing stock, companies also sell their stocks and buy the stocks of some other companies. This buying, however, is not restricted to companies only. Individuals also can participate in the stock selling and buying processes.

To a huge number of people, trading on stock markets seems to be a slightly risky, borderline gambling, speculative and for some people it may even seem that it is illegal in some sort. To be clear, there are legal regulations regulating the fair trading of stock markets and anything besides that is considered illegal. However, trading on stock markets is also far from being gambling because when you gamble your options may be reduced to all or nothing while on stock markets you do not get that kind of situation because you can always sell your stocks and even though you sold them for a less price than you bought them for you are still left with a certain amount of money, unlike in gambling.

One of the crucial things you need to know about the trading on stock markets is that you have to very familiar with what you are doing and everything related to the trading process of the stock of your interest. Trading on stock markets is very competitive and because of that always someone finishes as a winner and someone as a loser. In order to avoid being on the wrong side of the things, you should collect all data that you can about the stocks that you are planning to buy or sell.

One of the most common things that occur on stocks markets is a fluctuation of stock prices of certain companies. This happens due to the many factors. If that company is successful and had a good period of business, the price of its stock will be higher. However, if the companies had problems such as bad management, bad managing policies or some other type of scandal or misfortune, the price of its stocks will be lower. However, one of the most crucial factors that determine the value or the price of some stocks is the earnings of the given company.

On the other hand, the fluctuation of stock prices can be explained through a different approach as well. When the owners of a certain company are selling their stocks, and if there are more sellers than buyers it will happen that the price of the stock of that companies is lower. However, in the case when there are more buyers than sellers, the price of the stocks of that company will be higher because those buyers are competing by offer higher amount for a stock of the company and sellers are waiting and estimating when is the best time to sell the stocks and if they have reached a maximum price for the stocks.

One thing that can be said about the stock markets is that they are totally unpredictable. You can have a situation in which stocks of a certain company have had a high price for several years, and you decide to buy it thinking that it is a good investment and that it will bring you significant income. However, it can happen, that in very short period of time, the value of company's stocks drops and it leaves you in a situation where you are the owner of almost worthless stocks which results in you losing a fair amount of your money because nobody wants to buy those stocks or even if they buy it, they buy it for significantly less amount of money that you have previously spent in obtaining those stocks.

On the other hand, it can happen that you buy stocks of a certain company for a very small amount of money and then in a short period of time, the price of those stocks increases and it leaves you with a significant amount of money, much more than the amount for which you bought those stocks.

This leads us to another issue or rather to another question: What is the right time to buy stock? If you are in a position of waiting for the right price or the best price for you to buy stock it may happen that you missed the moment when the price was best for that.

Due to its unpredictability, it often happens that people wait for a lower price of stocks of certain companies in order to buy them and while doing that the price of a stock can go up, and you lost your opportunity to buy stocks at a lower price. The same is applicable to sellers as well. It can happen that when you are selling stocks that you wait for the highest offer but in that waiting for the stock price of your company can go down and in doing so it can create a situation where nobody wants to buy your stocks.

Often, it happens that the best time for selling the stocks is when other people at the stock markets are optimistic about their intentions, plans, expectations and trading results because all of this results in a high price of your stocks. Consequently, the best time to buy stocks perhaps is when others at stock markets are felling pessimistic about the prognoses, expectations, values, prices and the general situation on the stock market because in that case, the price of the stocks is low and that is the best time for you to buy those stocks.

The biggest mistake that happens in this context is when people decide to trade their stocks or chose a moment to sell them or buy them based on their emotions. Although, people who profited off that type of decision making in relation to stock trade will argue differently. As it is often the case, in the majority of cases we regret the decisions we made based on emotions and not looking at the broader picture or analyzing all available data.

With this being said it must be clear to you that in order to successfully trade on stock markets you need to be very well informed, you need to be able to process all relevant data on the issue and in some cases be ready for some risky moves which could pay off eventually. One way of earning money by owning stocks is when companies pay dividends to their owners. However, it must be emphasized that these dividends are not a law or regular thing. In the majority of cases, companies will not pay dividends to their stockholders, and those companies that pay may stop paying next year. This leaves stockholders with one way of earning money by owning stocks, and that is by selling these stocks again on the stock markets.

We can distinguish between two types of stocks: common and preferred stocks. When we talk about a common stock, we talk about the stocks that everybody is talking about and that are present in the majority of media reports.

Common stocks imply that you have a certain percentage of ownership in some company, and it gives you right for a certain percentage of the company's earnings. With common stocks, it happens sometimes that companies pay dividends to their owners, but that does not have to be a permanent source of income and it often happens that companies stop paying dividends to their stockholders. When you own a common stock of some company, you have a right to one vote in naming the members of the board as well.

However, on the other end of the spectrum are preferred stocks. The difference between common stocks and preferred stock is reflected mostly in dividend payment. In the majority of cases, if you own a preferred stock you will usually have a fixed payment of dividends for the rest of your life unlike it is the case with common stocks. Another advantage of preferred stock is the fact that in the case of bankruptcy of the company, the debt of the company towards you will be paid of much faster that it is the case with the owners of common stocks. One disadvantage of this type of stocks is the lack of voting rights that usually come with owning common stocks.

CHAPTER 9

STOCKS INVESTING TRICKS

Before investing in stocks, you need to educate yourself about it, so you can use your acquired knowledge intelligently and confidently. Furthermore, you need to be familiar with online resources that you can use to evaluate stocks and protect your profits. Ensure that you do your homework diligently before investing on stocks.

IMPORTANT CONSIDERATIONS ABOUT STOCKS INVESTING

In stock investing, note that you are not just buying stocks. You are actually buying an equitable share in a company. It is advisable to look for a profitable company where you can invest your money on. Make sure that this company has a high potential of becoming more profitable and successful in the future.

Also, note that you don't speculate by buying a company stock, which is not currently generating process. You don't also need to invest all your hard-earned money in stocks. Some seasoned investors also believe that there is a great chance for stocks to become more profitable during severe economic crisis.

It is also crucial to note that stock prices depend on the company's performance, the political status of the company, overall economic performance, the customers of the company, as well as the industry where your chosen company belongs to. The process of selecting stocks also requires logic and common sense. This is crucial in ensuring that you pick those that can provide you with the highest returns.

Knowing the reasons why you wish to invest in a particular stock is also crucial to your success. This is important during the stage when you are still analyzing whether that stock can benefit you.

Another thing that you have to consider is the need to use stop-loss orders if you are still unsure about the company's prospects. A stop-loss order is an order, which can trigger the automated system to sell the shares of stock upon meeting a particular requirement, like a particular stock price.

You also need to spend time monitoring the stocks and selling them if they are not performing well or if the economic conditions changed.

How to Check a Company's Fundamentals before Investing on its Stock?

Before investing in stocks, it is crucial to research about the companies that you want to be affiliated with. Pay close attention to the most important components of the company's financial statements including the following:

Earnings – Compare the company's earnings during the two most recent years. Last year's amount must be at least 10% higher than the one before it.

Sales – This amount must also be 10% higher than the one before it.

Debt – This amount must be lower or the same as the year before it. It must also be lower than the total assets of the company.

Equity – This amount must be higher than the previous year.

FINANCIAL FORMULAS TO LEARN BEFORE INVESTING IN STOCK

Price-to-Earnings (P/E) ratio – This ratio must be below 20 for large stocks and below 40 for all other stocks.

Price-to-Sales ratio (PSR) – This ratio must result to something closer to one.

Return on Equity – This number must be at 10% each year.

Earnings growth – Earnings must grow by at least 10% each year.

Debt-to-Asset Ratio – Debts must not be higher than 50% of the total assets.

READING LIST FOR ALL STOCK INVESTORS

Anyone who wants to invest in the stock market must spend time reading and doing his own research. It would be disastrous if you invest on a particular stock without knowing about the company beforehand. As such, spend time reading about the following:

- The annual report of the company
- The company filings with SEC, especially the 10K and 10Q reports
- S&P's Stock Reports
- Value Line Investment Survey

- Investor's Business Daily
- The Wall Street Journal

You can also check other reputable stock investing sites like Bloomberg, Financial Sense, King World News, Forbes, MarketWatch, NASDAQ, The Ludwig von Mises Institute, Yahoo Finance, and the US SEC.

REASSURANCE FOR NERVOUS STOCK INVESTORS

Stocks are volatile, therefore, you must aim to build your wealth while still maintaining peace of mind. Opt to invest in profitable companies with a growing customer base. Invest in companies that mainly cater to human needs, not wants. It is safer to diversify your portfolio, so you can include other profitable investments, as well.

Exert an effort to monitor your investment portfolio on a daily basis. Stay abreast with the general economy and the financial markets, so you can prepare for any eventuality. You should also learn how to use different investing tools, so you can control your investment accounts and gain more peace of mind. Lastly, be in control of your finances and debt, so you can lessen the pressure of investing aggressively over the short term.

Chapter 10

Important Things to Remember about Options Trading

Although both require careful study and research, options and stocks differ from each other. An individual who wants to trade options must know order types and indexes. It is also important to understand how the stocks affect options and indexes. Learning how to read stock market charts is also a key to success

Order Types

Market order – It is an order, which guarantees execution at the present market price because it has priority over the other order types.

Limit order – It is an order that does not guarantee execution but the price. It becomes a market order when the limit set by the investor is at least the present market ask price when buying, and there are contracts that can satisfy the order. In addition, it becomes a market order when the limit is at most the present market bid price when selling, and the available contracts can satisfy the order.

Stop order – It becomes a market order if the option price breaches a particular amount. You can use this strategy to minimize losses for an open position.

Stop-limit order – It becomes a limit order when option price meets the condition. However, this adds more risk because you may not be able to exit the option when you need to. The market may go against you when the price reaches the stop level.

Duration – The execution of the order will depend on two periods - the present trading session or the next session the market opens, and that time the investor or broker cancels the order.

Cancel or change – You can issue a cancel order if you want to cancel an active order. You will receive a notification about the cancellation after completing the instructions. You will also receive a notification if it is not possible to cancel the previous order because the cancel order came after the execution of the first. Note that you cannot cancel a market order.

A change order, on the other hand, is possible if you want to cancel the first order then make another order. You can also place a change order to replace an existing open order.

CHARTS AN OPTIONS TRADER CAN USE TO TRACK HIS INVESTMENTS

Line chart – It shows price versus time. The data points are single price for every period. A line connects these price points. The chart uses closing prices and offers information for trends and price movements by filtering out noise from the range data. It takes out the minor price moves. However, it does not offer information about the trading momentum during the day.

Open-High-Low-Close bar chart – It is also a price versus time chart. It shows the trading range as a vertical line while the horizontal tab on the left shows the open prices and the horizontal tab on the right shows the closing prices. It uses all the four prices and provides information about the price gaps and trading momentum.

Candlestick chart – It also shows the price versus time like the open-high-low-close chart. It is useful for daily analysis because you can see specific patterns that you can interpret to help you with your trading decision.

CONSTRUCTION OF FINANCIAL INDEXES

There are three ways to construct a financial index - price-weighted, market cap-weighted and equal dollar-weighted. The first one favors those stocks with higher prices while the second favors stocks with higher capitalizations. In the last method, no stock has an advantage over the others.

HOW STOCKS AFFECT INDEXES

A financial index measures prices for groups of stocks, commodities or bonds. If one stock changes, the change has an effect on the index. For example, a decline in a high-priced stock in a price-weighted index can have a bigger effect on an index than a decline in lower-priced stock.

On the other hand, a change in the market capitalization of a stock can affect a market-cap weighted index like the Standard & Poor's 500 index. For example, a change in Microsoft price can affect the S&P 500 even if the stock is trading at $30 per share because its capitalization is about $300 billion.

Each stock in an equal-dollar weighted index has similar effect on the value of the index. To keep the index balance, it is necessary to adjust the stock composition quarterly. This means that a particular stock with large gains for the last quarter can't have more weight on the index, thus, rebalancing has to take place.

CHAPTER 11

PRINCIPLES OF FUTURES TRADING

What actually happens when you buy futures? – is actually one of the most frequent questions in relation to futures trading. The answer to this question can be summarized in a sentence that states: when you buy futures you are actually accepting to buy products or services that the company from which you bought futures has not produced yet. In comparison to stock trading, future trading is much riskier because you deal with products and services that are not yet produced. With such characteristics, future trading is very popular not only among the producing companies and individuals and customers but also among speculators as well.

While stocks or shares are being traded on stock markets, futures are being traded on future markets. The idea of future markets developed from the needs of agricultural producers in mid-nineteenth century where often happened that the demand was much bigger than supply.

The difference between the future markets than and future markets today is that today's future markets have crossed the borders of agricultural production and entered many other sectors such as financial. As such, future markets today are used for buying and selling currencies as well as some other financial instruments. What future markets made possible is the opportunity for a farmer to be able to participate in the goods with customers on the other end of the world. One of the biggest and most important future markets is the International Monetary Market (IMM) that was established in 1972.

Futures are financial derivatives that obtain their value from the movement in price of another asset. It means that the price of futures is not dependent on its inherent value, but on the price of the asset the futures contract is tracking.

One of the advantages of future market is that is centralized and that people from around the world electronically are able to make future contracts. These future contract will specify the price of the merchandise and the time of delivery. Besides that, every future contract contains information about the quality and the quantity of the sold goods, specific price and the method in which the goods are to be delivered to the buyers.

A person who buys or sells a futures contract does not pay for the whole value of the contract. He pays a small upfront fee to trigger an open position. For example, if the value of the futures contract is $350,000 when the S&P 500 is 1400, he only pays $21,875 as its initial margin. The exchange sets this margin and may change anytime.

If the S&P 500 moved up to 1500, the futures contract will be worth $375,000. Thus, the person will earn $25,000 profit. However, if the index fell to 1390 from its original 1400, he will lose $2,500 because the futures contract will now be worth $347,500. This $2,500 is not a realized loss yet. The broker will also not require the individual to add more cash to his trading account.

However, if the index fell to 1300, the futures contract will be worth $325,000. The individual loses $50,000. The broker will require him to add more money to his trading account because his initial margin of $21,875 is no longer enough to cover his losses.

FUTURES MARKET CATEGORIES

There are similarities in all futures contracts. However, each contract may track different assets. As such, it is important to study the various markets that exist.

Categories of Futures Markets

Agriculture	Grains	Livestock	Dairy	Forest
Energy	Crude Oil	Heating oil	Natural gas	Coal
Stock Index	S&P 500	Nasdaq 100	Nikkei 225	E-mini S&P 500
Foreign Currency	Euro/USD	GBP/USD	Yen/USD	Euro/Yen
Interest Rates	Treasuries	Money markets	Interest Rate Swaps	Barclays Aggregate Index
Metals	Gold	Silver	Platinum	Base Metals

You can trade futures contracts on different categories and assets. However, if you are still a new trader, it is important to trade assets that you know. For example, if you are into stock trading for a few years already, you must start with futures contracts using stock indexes. This way, you won't have a hard time understanding the underlying asset. You only need to understand how the futures market works.

After choosing a category, decide on the asset that you want to trade. For example, you want trade futures contracts in the energy category. Focus on coal, natural gas, crude oil or heating oil. The markets trade at various levels, so you must understand relevant things, like the nuances, liquidity, margin requirements, contract sizes and volatility. Do the necessary research before trading in futures contracts.

TYPES OF TRADE

A basis trade allows you to go long or short on a futures contract and go short or long on the cash market. It is a wager that the difference in price between the two markets will fluctuate. For example, you decide to buy a 10-year US Treasury bond futures then sell a physical 10-year US Treasury bond.

A spread trade allows you to go short and long on two futures contracts. It is a wager that the difference in price between the futures contracts will change. For example, you buy an S&P 500 futures contract for August delivery and sell an S&P 500 futures contract for November delivery.

A hedging trade allows you to sell a futures contract to offset a position you hold in the current market. For example, a stock trader does not want to sell his shares for tax reasons. However, he is fearful of a sharp decline in the stock market so he sells S&P 500 futures contract as a hedge.

An important issue that must be mention in regards to futures and futures contracts is the notion of prices and the limits of future contracts. In future contracts, prices are expressed in classical currencies such as US dollars. The prices in the aspect of future contracts also have the minimum amount of money for which the price of the product may go up or go down. This minimum in the context of future contracts is referred to as "ticks". These tricks are very important for an investor who are investing huge sums of money or are buying a huge number of products because the fluctuation of prices can have enormous influence on the amount of money spent on certain products. It must also be noted that these "ticks" are not the same for each merchandise. Every commodity in the trading of futures has its own "ticks", the minimum for price fluctuation and it depends on the type of commodity.

CHAPTER 12

TRADING BITCOINS

Since the introduction of bitcoins in 2008, they have become a matter of controversies several times. These controversies resulted in bitcoins being banned in several countries including Bangladesh, China, Iceland, India, Bolivia, Sweden, Russia, Thailand and several others.

Bitcoin has been receiving a lot of bad press lately. It is a type of virtual money, which also serves as an alternative currency. Actually, it is more than mere currency. It is possible to buy bitcoin, but it is impossible to keep it in a piggy bank, under the mattress, or even in a regular bank account. Anyone who possesses bitcoins must secure them.

One of the main uses of bitcoins is for buying or paying things electronically. Since bitcoins are strictly digital currency they cannot be used in classical money transactions and with the very low amount of money paid for transaction costs, bitcoins became popular very quickly throughout the world.

BITCOIN BASICS

Satoshi Nakamoto developed Bitcoin as an alternative payment system in 2008. Bitcoin's purpose was to offer a decentralized, alternative, and viable financial infrastructure to the prevailing system. Bitcoin is a method of full and transparent spending through a block chain, a ledger that is publicly available. A transaction involves private and public keys.

One of the most important characteristics of bitcoins is the fact that bitcoin is a decentralized currency. This basically means that the bitcoin is not controlled by anyone or by any bank. Being decentralized, bitcoin is not subject to a constant change of values unlike it is the case with every other currency in the entire world. This also means that the users of bitcoins control their money themselves instead of some bank doing that for them.

While many currencies are based on the gold or silver, this is not the case with bitcoins. Bitcoins are based on the mathematical formula that is widely available, and it can be used by anyone.

Another advantage of bitcoin use is the fact that the transactions occur directly between users. Bitcoins are also a world currency. They can be used all over the world without calling your bank or even going to your bank to make changes to your account in order for you to use it in some foreign countries.

How to Buy Bitcoins?

Before you can use bitcoins, you need to know how it works exactly. Unfortunately, you cannot acquire some of them through conventional means. You need to buy them through a legitimate online platform like an exchange. You also need to register before you can use the platform, then you can deposit your local currency into the trading account then exchanges it to bitcoins based on the present exchange rate.

You can also buy physical bitcoins from another person. It is important to note that you possess the bitcoins, you need to take care of them like real money. It is not advisable to keep them in your online account for the long-term.

How to Store Bitcoins

Storage on an exchange is not secure. Some people even lost bitcoins from their exchange storage. It is best to use a software wallet, which allows you to secure your alternative currency on your own device. You can encrypt your own wallet and back it up on a separate device. However, your device must have good Internet security and virus checker.

You can also store your bitcoins on an online wallet while you are still on the stage of learning about them and their uses. Lastly, you can use a paper wallet to store the bitcoins to a particular bitcoin address not connected to software or online exchange. However, you can only spend them using a private key to redeem them manually.

How to Secure Bitcoins

You must secure your bitcoins in the same way you secure your personal bank account. Just like classical currencies, bitcoins are often subject to many wrongdoings by certain groups of people. Some unscrupulous groups and individuals may be interested in them. The password to open the bitcoins account must be unique. It is not good to use a common password for all your online accounts.

Just like it should be with any other password, your password for your bitcoin account should be regularly changed and in doing so, you should avoid obvious choices such as birthdays, important dates, phone numbers and similar things. Although it seems unnecessary to mention, it is very important not to share your account information with anyone unless you have a total trust in that person.

Even in that case, think again. Just like with real bank accounts you do not want for other people to have information that enables them to have full access to your accounts. One of the best ways of securing your bitcoins, as it was previously mentioned, is not to keep bitcoins too long in your account. In that way, you are depriving some groups of people of the opportunity to hack your account and stealing the funds from your account.

HOW TO MINE BITCOINS

Bitcoin mining uses state-of-the-art computers that can solve difficult equations. A bitcoin miner processes and confirms the transactions. It also creates new bitcoins and brings them into circulation.

The bitcoin network must be secure and robust. Individuals and institutions support it by dedicating computational power or running a bitcoin node. They also secure the network. You can mine bitcoins by using a 3rd party cloud-mining service or assembling your own rig. However, the last option requires expensive hardware.

Since the introduction of bitcoins into the world of money or currency, it became very quickly very popular. However, in recent years, we witness bitcoins keeping their popularity or even losing some of their popularity mostly because of the fact that bitcoins were used in some shady businesses conducted through the dark net.

Since bitcoins accounts do not require them to be connected with real life identity, that is, for accounts to have real names, bitcoins became popular among some criminal groups that misused them for their illegal activities. The notion of anonymity is very important aspects of bitcoins. When you use your bitcoin account or the address publicly then everyone else, meaning other users of bitcoins, can see how many bitcoins you have in your account but what they cannot see is to who does that account belongs to.

Bitcoins seem to be a future of money transactions because more and more people are seeing the benefits of having a currency not controlled by anyone but you and a currency that provides you with more privacy than real bank currency accounts. Bitcoins are proven so useful that even now in the USA, the Federal Reserves are recognizing the importance of such a notion and are introducing bitcoins as the currency of the future, and they are trying to incorporate bitcoins into the business of the banking sector.

Chapter 13

The Federal Reserves

The question of government interference in the sector economy for many people is a controversial issue because they think that governments should not interfere in the business and everything that goes with it. However, there are government bodies that regulation economic relation in the country and in such manner they protect the sector of the economy.

When we talk about the United States of America, the government body that regulates the issue of the economy is the Federal Reserve. The Federal Reserve is the bank of the United States of America and such it regulates all financial institutions present in the country. Since the Federal Reserve play such a crucial role in the economy of the USA and at the same time in the economy of the entire world, it is crucially important for all investors to be familiar with that institution and what it does.

Despite conducting business that regulates the most important aspect of even ordinary people, the Federal Reserve and its business was often under scrutiny which will be discussed in the following part of this chapter.

The Federal Reserve was created on December 23, 1913, by the United States Congress in order to introduce some level of control over the monetary issues in the country. The creation of this kind of financial institution was conducted mainly as an answer to a growing number of financial crises that occurred in the United States.

Since Congress is the founder of the Federal Reserve, it has the supreme authority over it, and all actions of the Federal Reserve are subject to the Congress oversight. It is important to mention that, despite being established by the government of the United States, the Federal Reserve, actually, is not part of the federal government establishment because creators wanted to preserve the independence and authority of this institution by depriving government officials of the direct power to control its businesses.

THE STRUCTURE

The Federal Reserve is located in the US capital, Washington D.C. The highest authority of the institution is the Board of Governors of the Federal Reserve. It consists of seven people appointed directly by the president of the USA and whose mandate last 14 years. It is important to emphasize that president cannot name the Board on its own because the names he suggests must be confirmed by the Senate and it also has a right of replacing the members of the Board. President also appoints the chairman and the vice-chairman of this institution for the period of 4 years.

The Federal Reserve has 12 regional branches or Federal Reserve Banks that are located across the country in different cities that can be classified as major cities. These regional branches or banks gain revenues in several ways. Some of those ways include income from providing different services to banks, earnings from holding foreign currency as well as interests in loans and government securities.

The Federal Reserve also has a branch that deals with policy making, and it is called the Federal Open Market Committee or FOMC.

The main responsibilities and duties of FOMC include making important decisions that influence interest rates and more importantly monetary policies. One final thing that is necessary to include in this part about the structure of the Federal Reserve is that all national banks are considered to be part of the Federal Reserve System.

DUTIES AND RESPONSIBILITIES

The Federal Reserve system controls all aspects of the economy, including levels of employment, economic growth, interest rates, and the value of the dollar. In other words, the main responsibility is to maintain our economy functioning without any evident interfering in the system itself.

There are no many differences between the duties and responsibilities of the 12 regional branches of the Federal Reserve in comparison to other banks. The only difference is that the Federal Reserve branches provide their services to different financial institutions while regular of commercial banks offer their service to individuals. The biggest client of the Federal Reserve is the United States government which may seem a bit ironic.

All the income collected by the United States Treasury are hosted by in the Federal Reserve system. During the time of World War II or during the Great Depression played the crucial role in lifting the United States out of crisis and enable the economy of US to grow rapidly. One of the most common practices inside the institution of the Federal Reserve that happen every once a while is the internal audits or the revisions of the operations that influence the status of the Federal Reserve.

This is conducted mainly for the reason of controlling their accounts and records are in order and that the principles set forth by the Federal Reserve are respected fully. Besides this kind, inside, revision all branches of the Federal Reserve are subject to additional revisions and controls by external factors in the first place by a government authority that oversights this institution.

One of the most important functions of the Federal Reserve is the possibility of that system to provide the US government with the steady source of loans and credits. Besides this, the entire financial system is under the control and management of this institution. The Federal Reserve can be characterized as one big bank that directs and controls the smaller banks and as such, it has the capacity and the means to loan funds to member banks, in fact, 12 of them as it was previously mentioned.

One of the functions connected to the business of the Federal Reserve is the determination of the requirements that all bank reserve must have which can be characterized as a proportion of the amount of the total deposits that other banks in the country must have in their accounts that are available to those banks in the form of liquid cash. Also, in recent years a shift in the definition of the Federal Reserve's function occurred.

In the recent period, the Federal Reserve has become an institution that lends its financial means as a last resort in order to save some financial institutions that are on the verge of bankruptcy. This new role of the Federal Reserve System reflects the need of saving such financial institution and also indicate how serious consequences may the bankruptcy of such financial institution have on the country's economy and on the people as well.

Besides that, the Federal Reserve also plays an important role in the creation, adaptation and maintenance of the monetary policies of the United States of America. With this being said and knowing the fact that the United States economy is the leading economy in the world and that it dictates trends in the world's economy, the importance of the Federal Reserve is raised from the level of the US to the level of the world. Consequently, the Federal Reserve dictates trends in the world's economy as well and every decision made by the Board of Governors of the Federal Reserve reflects on the world economy.

Monetary policy in its definition refers to the actions conducted by different financial institutions, firstly the Federal Reserve, and some government institutions in relations to the amount of money in circulation. The goal of such policies, according to the definition, is to boost the country's economy, ensure the growth of the country's economy, make employment of people possible and maintain the prices of interest rates and other issues related to the financial sector.

CONTROVERSIES

Among all of these functions of this financial institution, several controversies arose in relation to the business of the institution. One of such controversies happened when it was revealed that one function of this institution is to receive money transfers from the US Treasury, and after it has received it, this institution would later distribute this money to regional banks that are the members of the Federal Reserve. From all of this, we can conclude that the Federal Reserve serve as a middleman in transferring a huge amount of money to regional banks.

Since its creation, the Federal Reserve has been criticized, and the necessity of such institution has been debated since the first day of its establishment. There are even those people who claim that the Federal Reserve and all the business it is conduction is unconstitutional, and they are calling for the abolishment of such institutions. These kinds of debates even led to splitting into major parties on the political scene of the United States in the time when George Washington's administration controlled government institutions. In the more recent period, some United States congressmen have called for a stricter approach towards the Federal Reserve as well as establishing a more efficient control over the doings of such financial institution.

The main issue that these congressmen are raising is related to the amount of power that the Federal Reserve has acquired during the last 100 years and the role that this institution had in decision making in the Congress and the Senate. Another important controversial issue in relation to this institution is the matter of who owns this institution.

The official website of the Federal Reserve offers an explanation that this institution is not a privately owned corporation. However, since the role of the government authorities has been reduced to a minimum, the question remains who actually controls the business of this institution and for whom are the Board members doing while they make decisions that impact millions of people. Additionally, 100 percent of the shareholders of the Federal Reserve are private, commercial banks and as such this institution is clearly a privately owned organization. Another statement that can be found on official website of this institution says that this institution is a non-profit institution. However, this statement also proves to be controversial since the amount of money located in the accounts of this institution tells different stories.

So one may wonder how does this system of the Federal Reserve affects ordinary people and their everyday life. Let's say that you are looking to buy a home or a new car. In order to do so, you have to get a loan from the bank because your current funds are just not enough. When getting a loan from the bank, your final contract will contain several segments on something called interest rates.

Since the interest rates have been explained in previous parts of this book, we will not bother you again with explaining what interest rates are. What is important for you to know is that the amount of money that you will have to return to the bank is much higher if the interest rates are high and much smaller if the interest rates are lower. Consequently, in order for banks not to give you enormous interest rates, the Federal Reserve determines the maximum and minimum level of the amount of interest rates for different type of bank loans. In doing so, the Federal Reserve prevents commercial and other banks from making huge amounts of money from the interest rates given on different types of loans.

With all this being said it is clear that the role of the Federal Reserve influences all aspects of the financial sector of the United States and the world as well. It does not only influence financial institutions, but it also influences the lives of ordinary people because its decisions and regulations are mostly felt by ordinary people. Despite being surrounded by so many controversies in its more than 100-year-old history, the significance of such institution is tremendous, and it begs the question what will happen if certain congressmen succeed in their goal of abolishing this institution. This move can prove to be critical, and it can lead to another crush of financial institutions like the one that happen in 1930 or more recently in 2008.

With the issue of ownership still not fully resolved one cannot but wonder what are the true intentions of such institution and for whom it is working. Established by the people of the United States in order to provide them with the security of financial sector in a time when financial crises happened regularly, the Federal Reserve seemed to have lost their creator's intentions and turned their focus on the more cooperative based economy.

Chapter 14

Lessons From Mutual Funds and University Endowments

One of the best ways to learn a new skill is by observing experts. This is true for technical trades, for sports, for music...and, it also holds true in the world of investing. If you hope to gain a deeper understanding of the moves you need to take in order to secure your financial future, you need to take time to study the strategies of those who have come before you and succeeded. In this chapter, we will briefly explore the logic and reasoning behind some of the most successful strategies out there -- offering you insight into the decisions that you are bound to face as an investor yourself.

Mutual Funds

Because you are reading this ebook, it is pretty safe to assume that you are making a serious effort to educate yourself about investing -- and if you are educating yourself about investing, it is a pretty safe bet that you have heard the word "diversification" about a million times.

You probably even understand why diversification is so important. Imagine one investor who placed all his money in oil stocks. Now imagine an investor who places a third of her money in oil stocks, a third in green energy stocks, and a third in non-energy related stocks. It should be pretty easy to see who has a safer portfolio.

The investor who placed all his money in oil will be completely dependant upon oil prices, which can be extremely volatile. If a major reserve is found, a brilliant new clean energy source discovered, or if foreign affairs wreck havoc on oil prices, all the savings that this investor has in the world could be wiped out overnight.

The investor who placed a portion of her money in oil stocks and a portion in green tech, on the other hand, will sleep a bit better at night. She knows that any dramatic change in oil stocks will likely be offset by an inverse shift in the price of green tech. And should the energy sector itself experience a downturn, she knows that a substantial amount of her money is invested in other sectors of the economy.

Of course, this example in itself is a drastic oversimplification of what effective diversification really looks like. Owning stock in just two sectors of the economy is not exactly an utterly fail safe way of protecting against a rainy day. In fact, a truly diversified portfolio would likely contain hundreds of stocks from dozens of industries.

How can your average Joe afford such a thing? Even if you had a million dollars to invest, you would be unable to attain this level of diversification! This is exactly where mutual funds come into the picture.

Mutual funds function in exactly the way that the name would imply: they consist of one large collective fund that hundreds of investors contribute to. They are managed by teams of experts who take advantage of this enormous pool of money to build a highly diversified portfolio, all while taking advantage of lower overhead costs associated with bulk purchasing.

There are two important lessons that you should take away from this discussion of mutual funds. First of all, placing some of your own investment money into a mutual fund is a great way to diversify your own portfolio and add some low-risk sources of growth to your income. Secondly, when constructing the rest of your portfolio, you should still take into account the power that diversification offers, and make an effort to offset your risks in order to build toward long-term success.

University Endowments

It may surprise you to learn that some of the best "investors" in the country (in fact, in the world) are the prestigious private and public schools of the United States. First and foremost among the examples of this is Harvard University, whose endowment has been grown to a whopping 35 billion dollars!

Harvard certainly isn't alone, either. Yale, the University of Texas, Princeton, and Stanford also enjoy well over 20 billion dollars a peice in endowment funds. In part, as you might imagine, this has to do with the wealthy donors who give money to those school. It certainly makes sense: smart, oftentimes wealthy people attend prestigious schools, use that prestige (and perhaps their previous family wealth) to become enormously successful themselves, and then they give back to the universities that helped make them who they are.

This cycle of donations certainly helps, but it isn't the whole story. These universities don't only enjoy big endowments because they have received lots of donations, they enjoy substantial endowments because the money that they have received has been well managed.

This is actually where the success of former students plays its biggest role. When a school such as Yale decides to hire managers for its endowment, it has one of the most impressively talented bases of highly motivated and personally involved job applicants to chose from: it's own former students! The sheer talent with which university endowments are managed is what helps them attain success.

So, what lesson can you, a humble investor, take from all this? First of all, management matters. When you choose a mutual fund, pay close attention to who is managing it and what track record that person boasts. The manager of your mutual fund literally has your financial future in his or her hands, so don't give the job to just anyone! Sometimes, paying a bit more in fees is worth the extra growth that your money can achieve when you work with someone who is truly qualified.

Additionally, it is worthwhile to take a look at how these funds are managed. Unfortunately, most universities are actually not required to disclose any information regarding their own endowment portfolios, meaning that gleaning any details from these investment experts is difficult. However, there is some information that we do have access to -- the most consequential of which is probably the percentage of the endowments that universities spend each year. Despite the many financial needs that prestigious universities encounter, they typically spend less than 5% of their endowments each year -- ensuring that growth from their investments will outpace spending. This is a prerequisite for continued growth, and personal investors would do well to follow such a model in their own investing lives.

Chapter 15

Good Debt Vs. Bad Debt

Living debt-free your entire life may seem like a valiant goal, but the truth is that it can be a destructive objective to pursue. Many of the most important and empowering purchases that you will make over the course of your life are simply too expensive for that vast majority of people to purchase with a savings account. Paying for university, purchasing a car, or buying your first home, for example, are all likely to require a bit of credit, even if you are doing quite well for yourself financially. So, in order to help guide you through the process of taking on debt -- without limiting your options from the future more than is absolutely necessary -- we have compiled this chapter as a brief guide to debt. After all, managing debt correctly is a necessity for anyone who hopes to invest a portion of their income in the future.

In fact, as long as you have your debts under control, there is nothing wrong with spending your extra income on investments rather than making extra payments in order to pay your loans down quicker. A direct subsidized loan for students, for example, has an average APR of under 5%, which can be outpaced relatively easily with smart investments on the stock market.

Moreover, understanding your debts now will help you build the credit that you may need in the future to help you children get funded for important expenditures such as University, which will come at a point in their lives when they still have yet to build credit of their own. In the next chapter, we will discuss another important element of ensuring a solid financial future for your children: educating them about personal finances. For now, let's take a quick look at the most important distinguishing factors between good and bad debt.

KEY CHARACTERISTICS OF GOOD DEBT

- **Good debt has the potential to offer financial returns or generate future income.** Student debt is a good example of this. The average college grad earns roughly one million dollars more than a non-grad over the course of their life, so taking on a few thousand dollars in debt in order to attain this goal is well worth it.
- **Good debt comes at a low interest rate.** This is why ultra-low-interest loans made to entrepreneurs in developing countries constitute good debt for the business people in question, not predatory lending practices by the government or charity institutions implementing them.
- **Good debt can also be tax deductible.** There are two key benefits to this: first of all, the obvious savings. Because the government encourages homeownership, for example, the interest on mortgages is tax deductible, which makes things easier on people who buy their own homes. Secondly, debt that achieves tax-deductible status is more likely to be for a positive and growth-creating cause.

KEY CHARACTERISTICS OF BAD DEBT

- **Bad debt does not offer potential for the future.** Taking out a loan to fund your dream wedding might seem like a good idea, but it offers no real benefits for the future, and it will force you to begin your marriage in debt! Many forms of bad debt are based upon a desire for instant gratification, so learning to delay rewards (i.e. agreeing to go on that dream vacation for your one year anniversary instead) is an important skill.

- **Bad debt comes at a high interest rate.** You have probably heard a horror story or two in your time about people who took out a payday loan thinking it would be a good way to get through a tough week, only to end up trapped in a vicious cycle of compounding debt. The reason why payday loans are so dangerous? They have very high interest rates.
- **Bad debt is almost never tax deductible.** Good luck convincing the IRS to subsidize a high interest payday loan or a loan attached to a frivolous expense!

Now that you know the basics, you will be able to manage your credit and debt more coherently, leading to long-term wealth and more buying power in the future.

CHAPTER 16

TEACHING YOUR CHILDREN ABOUT MONEY

One of the most important elements of helping your children plan for success while security your own financial legacy is to teach your kids about money. Unfortunately, many otherwise intelligent and involved parents fall short when it comes to this critical task.

There are several reasons for this, as we will see throughout this chapter -- but one of the most important reasons why this occurs is that many parents believe that they can allow schools to impart this knowledge. This is completely false: first of all, there is no nationally mandated curriculum regarding personal finance, and many schools offer sub-par financial education, opt-in financial education, or no financial education at all. Secondly, even if your children's school is teaching them about finance, you as a parent need to lend an important helping hand.

So, if you have children, or plan on having children someday in the future, this chapter can help you better understand the role that you need to play in their own education. Even if having a child isn't yet on your radar, or if you don't plan on having kids, this chapter still may be worth a look -- the odds are good that your own financial education lacked a few important points, and taking a moment to analyze the shortcomings of financial education could help you develop a more well-rounded understanding of your own knowledge.

To begin this chapter, we will review a few of the reasons why schools tend to avoid imparting a thorough understanding of personal finances to their students. In the second section, we will argue that no school -- no matter how esteemed -- can offer *all* the financial education that a young student needs. And in the third and final section of this chapter, we will offer a few easy-to-implement guidelines for giving your children a solid understand of how finances work.

WHY ISN'T PERSONAL FINANCE TAUGHT IN SCHOOL?

First of all, let's take a quick look at a few of the most important reasons why financial education is not given the emphasis it deserves as a crucial life skill:

- **The Factory Model of Education.**
  This term is often repeated by financial experts, education professionals, and political activists -- but what exactly does it mean? The idea of factory model education was first developed in the 1800's, and, to be fair, it made a lot of sense at the time. Industrializing countries around the world were eager to use their newfound economic development to further education, and for this reason mandatory public education was instituted in places such as Prussia, France, Great Britain, and, eventually, the United States.

How were industrializing countries to handle this enormous influx of new students? By using a highly efficient, industrial model, of course! Students were to be treated much like objects on an assembly line, passing from one identical classroom to the next, each receiving the same one-size-fits-all instruction. Not only did this method promise to educate the masses in a uniform and cost-effective way, it also promised to create an ideal workforce for the industrial industry that drove the world economy at the time. Students would leave the educational system knowing how to take orders, perform simple and repetitive tasks, and complete work in a timely manner. What else would your average Joe need>

The modern economy has changed enormously. Our hopes and dreams as human beings have changed enormously. But sadly, our school system hasn't changed all that much. All across the country, children leave the education system without acquiring basic skills -- and financial education is oftentimes one of the items not incorporated into our outdated approach to education.

- **Lack of Student/Parent Interest.**
To be fair, not all the blame can be placed directly on "the system." There are many private and charter schools around that do not place emphasis on financial education, either. Moreover, most public school curriculums are determined by local school boards -- which tend to be very democratically-run and responsive to the opinions of the local population. Yet schools have still not adapted. Why? A simple question of supply and demand.

For example, you have probably heard a story or two about how local students and parents banded together to stand up to the city and convince the school board to protect funding for a music or art program. There's nothing wrong with that, of course -- in fact, studies have shown that participation in any extracurricular activity, regardless of how pragmatic that activity may be, tends to greatly boost students' chances for success later in life. The problem is simply that parents and students do not take the same initiative when it comes to financial education. Although learning about the basics of personal finance might not be as exciting as taking guitar lessons or playing football, it is highly important, and should be prioritized just as much.

- **(Perceived) Lack of Universal Applicability**
  Some schools may also be hesitant to implement financial education into their curriculums because they worry that the same financial concepts may not be universally applicable to all students. For example, students from a certain background might be far more concerned with learning how to apply for FAFSA, whereas students from a different background might be more concerned with purchasing a new car or helping out in the family business. Therefore, schools shy away from teaching about finances because they worry that the subjects studied might bore, frustrate, or even create division between students.

  Unfortunately, this is a tremendous wasted opportunity. First of all, there is always value in learning a new skill, even if that skill may not appear immediately useful. For example, it is the students who come from humble backgrounds without experience managing large amounts of money who will most need the skills they could be developing in such a class. Likewise, even students who don't plan on filing FAFSA may someday wish to help out a relative, or they may even find themselves filing for a grant someday in the future and wish that they had experience in the field. Last but not least, such an education is just as much of an opportunity to create mutual respect and understanding as it is to create division -- controversy is a natural and healthy part of any solid education, and it is not something that should be avoided.

WHAT ABOUT THE GOOD SCHOOLS?
- **The Financial Industry**
  Last but not least, it is an undeniable reality that the financial industry itself has lobbied hard to keep financial education out of schools. The sad truth is that there are many people and institutions poised to benefit financially from the debt in which new generations may find themselves -- and in this sense, the less that today's students understand their own finances, the more money that these financial institutions can take in. This is precisely why parents must take matters into their own hands and work hard to impart smart financial values to their children!

"Okay," you might say, rather defensively, "obviously there are a lot of problematic schools out there, but my kids attend a top-tier institution that values pragmatic skills!"

Clearly, children who attend such schools are far more likely to develop the skills that they will need in order to attain and sustain financial success. However, it is important to understand that children are far more likely to succeed when this education is backed up by hands-on parenting that reinforces the important points learned in school.

Even if your child's school does feature a comprehensive course (or two) on financial education, you cannot guarantee that the information presented in this course will be complete, or even completely accurate. After all, the curriculum to your child's course could be flawed for any of the same reasons that were mentioned above -- perhaps the teacher or the institution is biased; perhaps lobbying or a fear of controversy has caused certain items to be left out of the course.

More to the point: even if the personal finance courses that your child takes are perfect, they are not going to impart *values* as effectively as you, the parent, could. This is perhaps the most important point in this entire chapter: the information that your child receives in any financial education course will ultimately be meaningless unless that information is remembered, valued, and implemented.

How can this be achieved? Most experts agree that the best way to teach kids to really live by the principles of smart financial practices is by making this education a part of your life style. Think about it: no one in their right minds would think that a one-time chat about math, literature, music, or biology would be enough to impart a real understanding of these subjects to their kids -- so why would you think that talking once or twice about smart financial management would be enough, either?

How can parents help teach children these principles? In the final section of this chapter, we will offer some concrete details that can help you get started.

TIPS FOR EFFECTIVELY TEACHING YOUR CHILDREN ABOUT FINANCES

- **Give a weekly allowance.** Starting with grade school, a weekly allowance is a great way to help kids practice using and managing money. Over time, it will allow them to experience the consequences of their financial choices in a variety of low-pressure ways. They will, surely, spend all their money at once on an unfortunate purchase or two -- and, if encouraged, they will also try saving. The idea of this is to ensure that they make mistakes when it doesn't matter, that they practice developing good habits, and that they get comfortable managing their own money.
- **Tie allowance to household chores.** This concept is bit controversial -- there are many parents who would argue that children should not view collaborating in the home as a "job," but rather as an inherent part of being a family. Nonetheless, there are many positive aspects to allowing your children to work for their allowance: it teaches them the value of hard work, it gives extra motivation to complete their household duties, and it helps drive home the point that "money doesn't grow on trees." Our recommendation: give your kids certain chores that are simply responsibilities, such as keeping their room clean and washing the dishes. However, offer the chance to earn an allowance completing extra chores: i.e. taking out the trash or washing the car. You could even offer special one-time gigs such as "clean out the old bookshelf in the spare room." The idea, once again, is to create a space where children can learn and practice financial management without the pressure or consequences that they will have to deal with later in life.
- **Don't shy away from talking about money.** Many parents are hesitant when it comes to speaking with their kids about their own finances -- and although it obviously isn't a good idea to share *everything,* the truth is our squeamishness about finances can create a feeling of taboo

that causes unhealthy attitudes toward money. The truth is that kids pick up on more than you realize anyway, and it is better to be open and share in order to help kids understand the choices that they will need to make later in life. Your own triumphs, failures, insights, and opinions can be enormously useful to your kids, so sharing them (in an age-appropriate way, obviously,) is a good decision.

- **Analyze costs and benefits.** One way to give your kids everyday insights into making better financial decisions is to discuss the costs and benefits of certain purchases when the opportunity arises. This could be as simple as asking them to compare cereal prices in order to discover that buying generic brands, and/or buying in larger quantities can result in big savings. Or it could be as complex as talking about why you chose to purchase your home among all the other homes that you considered. Once again, a bit of common sense and discretion are important, as an eight year old and a sixteen year old are going to have entirely different capacities to understand such decisions.

- **Discuss the benefits of a savings fund.** A great chat topic next time you go to the bank: the importance of savings. For a young child, this could be as simple as letting them know that the bank is a place where you can save money that you have already earned. and not a place where you can go to receive free money. (This is a good place for a joke about the over-availability of credit, but we'll save that subject for the next bullet point!) An older child may be ready to learn about simple concepts such as interest, or the difference between a checking account and a savings account. And a high schooler may be ready to weigh the security of saving money in a relatively low-growth interest account versus the extra potential of investing that same money in the stock market. (Once again, we've touched upon a topic that we'll come back to here in a minute -- talking to your kids about investing is an often-overlooked aspect of financial education, but it is critical. As you have hopeful begun to understand in the course of reading this book, investing is one of the most effective ways of building long-term wealth.) Be sure to emphasize the distinct benefits of having a savings fund: in addition to the compounding interest that the bank offers, those who make a savings fund for themselves have the security of knowing that they will be prepared if and when a rainy day arrives, and they will also be able to avoid purchasing as much on credit...which brings us to our next point.

- **Introduce the concept of debt and credit.** It's a simple fact of life: using credit is almost certainly going to be necessary at some point or another. More importantly, it will be offered to your children constantly throughout their adult lives, whether they need it or not. There are many factors in our society driving people to take out too much debt. The high cost of education, the notion that a four year university is a must, the need for housing and transportation, predatory lenders, the need to 'keep up with the Joneses, and so many other aspects of modern life will push your kids toward over-using their credit cards and taking out loans -- it is your job to help them understand that credit is not "free money." On the other end of the spectrum, there are a growing number of people who take the opposite approach, avoiding credit at all cost -- right up until the point where they want to purchase a home or a car, only to find that they have not built up a solid enough credit record to get that project funded! By talking to your children about the benefits and risks of credit, and stressing the importance of living within your means, you can help your kids develop a healthy and intelligent attitude toward debt.

- **Talk about investing.** Last but not least, you should teach your kids how to make their money work for them. So many people spend their entire lives working in order to build their net worth without ever taking advantage of the powerful opportunities that the stock market has to offer. Sharing the concept of investing can be simple, easy, and even fun -- and, as your kids grow older, you may even wish to discuss a few of your own investments. Most experts recommend teaching through examples, not through 'cold hard data,' because kids (and people in general) tend to remember stories far better than they remember equations. In other words, feel free to share the concepts that you learn in this ebook; but be sure to illustrate them with examples from your own life and from the real world!

To end this chapter, it is fitting to stress once again the importance of making financial education a regular part of your life. Our personal finances are, in many ways, a result of our own day-to-day choices, habits, and lifestyle, and teaching them in a way that reflects this reality is the best way to help your kids prepare for a brighter future.

CHAPTER 17

THE FUTURE IS YOURS!

Congratulations! The learning journey that we have undertaken with this e-book is drawing to a close, and the real adventure -- building your personal wealth -- is about to begin.

If you have made it this far in our book, the odds are good that you are truly serious about taking control of your financial life. At this point, it should be pretty clear why the "traditional" path to wealth simply isn't going to cut it.

On television and radio, in magazines and newspaper advertisements, financial advisors all preach the same manipulative message about personal finances. They tell you to go to school and study a profession that carries a nice and reliable income. They tell you to put 10% of your earnings into a savings account, and to penny-pinch the joy out of your life by cutting back on life's finer pleasures. They tell you to invest in liabilities such as your home and your car. They tell you that you can "beat the market" with a million unproven and financially risky investments. And the reward they promise? The ability to retire into the sunset when you yourself are already in the sunset of your life!

This strategy is based upon waiting and uncertainty -- two things that simply don't go well together. With a smart and active approach to investing, you can begin building and enjoying your wealth now -- opening the door to a better life for yourself and your family.

Here's the problem with all of these high-energy talk show hosts, slick-talking advertisements, and wild promises: they are oftentimes selling a pipe dream of 'beating the market.'

The smarter move, as unexciting as it may be in the present moment, is to build a diversified range of investments that will carry you toward financial stability regardless of the ups and downs of the world economy.

A zero-sum game is defined as any endeavor in which there are clear winners and losers. Mathematically speaking, a true zero sum game implies that each and every gain is perfectly balanced by an equal loss, and vice versa. Trying to beat the stock market is in itself a perfect example of a zero sum game. For every person who manages to guess ahead and outsmart those who rely on existing trends, there is another person who failed to accomplish that and lost out. Do you really want to trust your financial future to such a volatile system? Moreover, there are many costs associated with the rapid fire maneuvering of stocks that is required to even *attempt* to outsmart the market. You can expect to pay more taxes, more fees, and spend a whole lot more of your personal time staring at stock prices on a computer screen, for example. Once all of this is taken into account, it becomes clear that attempting to beat the market is not even a zero sum game, it is a loser's game.

Holding a diverse range of the nation's' publicly owned businesses over an extended period of time, on the other hand, is not a zero sum game at all. The world economy is constantly growing and expanding, and everyone who has a generalized stake in the economy is bound to enjoy being alone for this ride.

With the information that you have gained in this ebook, you will now have a functional understanding of how to ensure that you can be along for the ride -- and, just as importantly, you will have the skills needed to manage, sustain, and grow your newfound wealth.

Our parting message: the future is yours! You have what it takes to make your financial dreams come true, all that is missing now is action. Good luck, and be sure to refer back to these pages whenever you need a guiding hand in your new and exciting endeavors!

Conclusion

Thank you again for downloading this book!

I hope this book was able to help you to learn about some of the most relevant investing concepts.

The next step is to get your feet wet and apply what you learned into your life.

Finally, if you enjoyed this book, then I'd like to ask you for a favor, would you be kind enough to leave a review for this book on Amazon? It'd be greatly appreciated!

Click here to leave a review for this book on Amazon!

Thank you and good luck

FREE BONUS: "Click The Link Below To Receive Your Bonus

https://publishfs.leadpages.co/pangea-health/

www.ingramcontent.com/pod-product-compliance
Lightning Source LLC
Chambersburg PA
CBHW060349190526
45169CB00002B/535